W9-CRZ-472

People Around the World

Life and Culture in
SOUTHWEST
ASIA
AND NORTH
AFRICA

MIRIAM COLEMAN

PowerKiDS
press.

Published in 2021 by The Rosen Publishing Group, Inc.
29 East 21st Street, New York, NY 10010

First Edition

Editor: Siyavush Saidian
Book Design: Seth Hughes

Photo Credits: Cover pp. 5, 45 dikobraziy/Shutterstock.com; p. 7 Claude Zygiel/Wikimedia Commons; p. 8 AP Photo/Emrah Gurel) p. 9 (left) Roman Debree/Shutterstock.com; p. 9 (right) GALI TIBBON/Contributor/AFP/Getty Images; p. 11 (top) AP Photo/Mosa'ab Elshamy) p. 11 (bottom) AHMAD GHARABLI/Contributor/AFP/Getty Images; p. 13 ATTA KENARE/Contributor/AFP/Getty Images; p. 15 (left) MAHMOUD KHALED/Contributor/AFP/Getty Images; p. 15 (right) leshiy985/Shutterstock.com; p. 16 JACK GUEZ/Staff/AFP/Getty Images; p. 17 THOMAS COEX/Contributor/AFP/Getty Images; p. 19 AP Photo/Kamran Jebreili; p. 20 (left) Ilia Yefimovich/picture-alliance/dpa/AP Images; p. 20 (right) AP Photo/Amr Nabil; p. 22 AP Photo/Ebrahim Noroozi; p. 23 BANDAR ALDANDANI/Contributor/AFP/Getty Images; p. 26 STEPHANE DE SAKUTIN/Staff/AFP/Getty Images; p. 27 AP Photo/Amr Nabil); p. 28 AP Photo/Ebrahim Noroozi p. 30 AP Photo/ Tara Todras-Whitehill; p. 31 AP Photo/Raad/Adayleh; p. 32 Heritage Images/Contributor/Hulton Fine Art Collection/Getty Images; p. 34 Artography/Shutterstock.com; p. 35 (top) VW Pics/Contributor/Universal Images Group/Getty Images; p. 35 (bottom) JACK GUEZ/Staff/AFP/Getty Images; p. 36 PAUL ATKINSON/Shutterstock.com; p. 38 STRINGER/Stringer/AFP/Getty Images; p. 40 AP Photo/Amr Nabil; p. 42 (AP Photo/stf; p. 43 (top) AP Photo/Manoocher Deghati; p. 43 (bottom) AP Photo/Hasan Jamali; p. 44 Ton Koene/picture-alliance/dpa/AP Images.

Cataloging-in-Publication Data

Names: Coleman, Miriam.
Title: Life and culture in Southwest Asia and North Africa / Miriam Coleman.
Description: New York : PowerKids Press, 2021. | Series: People around the world | Includes glossary and index.
Identifiers: ISBN 9781725321687 (pbk.) | ISBN 9781725321700 (library bound) | ISBN 9781725321694 (6 pack) | ISBN 9781725321717 (ebook)
Subjects: LCSH: Middle East–Juvenile literature. | Middle East–Social life and customs–Juvenile literature. | Middle East–Social conditions–Juvenile literature.
Classification: LCC DS44.C65 2021 | DDC 956–dc23

Manufactured in the United States of America

Find us on

Contents

Introduction

AN AREA OF MANY NAMES AND PLACES

Southwest Asia and North Africa is a vast region that stretches from Morocco in the west to Afghanistan in the east, and from the Mediterranean and Black Seas in the north to the Indian Ocean in the south. The region is known by many names. It's often referred to as the Arab world, though not all people in this region are Arabs. It's also sometimes called the Islamic world, though not all its people are Muslims. There are far more Muslims living outside of this area, especially in South Asia and Southeast Asia. Most people today call this region the Middle East, or the Middle East and North Africa

This map of southwest Asia and North Africa shows the region's position as a bridge connecting Africa, Asia, and Europe.

(MENA)—although this geographic description comes from a Western European point of view.

It can be a hard region to pin down, since its borders are based on both culture and geography. The region is generally thought to include 19 countries with a combined population of around 381 million people. This amounts to 6 percent of the world's population. Though the region has seen political unrest and dangerous wars in recent decades, it's also a land of deep religious and cultural traditions that have spread far and wide across the globe.

1
MANY PEOPLES, MANY LANGUAGES

Southwest Asia and North Africa lie at a crossroads of continents and cultures. The region's location at the meeting point of Africa, Asia, and Europe—along with its history of trade routes and exploration—has given it a rich mix of peoples. This **diversity** of **ethnicities** is reflected in the languages spoken in the region.

CULTURAL CONNECTIONS

Many countries in the region still show the influence of the European countries that once occupied them— especially that of France in Algeria and Tunisia, Britain in Egypt and Yemen, and Italy in Libya.

diversity: Exhibiting a variety of types.
ethnicity: A group that shares common cultural traits, such as language.

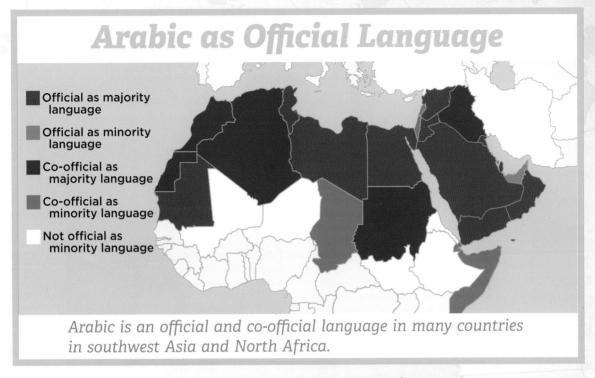

Arabic as Official Language

- Official as majority language
- Official as minority language
- Co-official as majority language
- Co-official as minority language
- Not official as minority language

Arabic is an official and co-official language in many countries in southwest Asia and North Africa.

The language spoken most in the region is Arabic, which comes from the Arab ethnic group. Arabs and their language originated in the Arabian Peninsula and spread throughout much of southwest Asia and North Africa through successful military conquests beginning in the mid-sixth century. Even within the Arab ethnic and language group, there's a great deal of diversity. There are some 35 different **dialects** of Arabic spoken across the region, and speakers of one dialect can't always understand another.

A Stateless People

One of the largest ethnic minority groups in the region, the Kurds have significant communities in Iran, Iraq, Syria, and Turkey, making up 7 to 20 percent of the populations of those countries. They currently have no nation of their own, but many Kurds have long sought to create an **autonomous** Kurdish state, at times participating in armed conflict to establish it. Others are only seeking equal rights, such as recognition of their distinct language and identity, and autonomy within other nations. In 1946, a Kurdish independent state existed for a brief time within Iran, and the Kurds currently have self-rule in northern Iraq.

Kurdish women in Istanbul, Turkey, celebrate the Kurdish New Year.

While most people in most countries in this region speak Arabic, there are a few exceptions. Most people in Iran are Persian, not Arab, and they mostly speak Farsi (also known as Persian), a language related to Kurdish and Armenian. Most people in Turkey are Turkish—also not Arab—and the Turkish language is in a family of its own.

A paste made from smashed chickpeas, hummus is a food common to nearly every country in the region.

Large numbers of Ethiopian Jews began migrating to Israel in 1977, forming a distinct community. Ethiopian Jews are shown here celebrating the holiday Sigd.

Israel's population includes a large Arab minority, but the majority are Jews of various ethnicities, including a large group with European ethnic roots. The primary language of Israel's Jewish population is Hebrew, which comes from the same language family as Arabic.

CULTURAL CONNECTIONS

Israel's Jewish population is made up of many different groups. Ashkenazi Jews immigrated mostly from Europe and America, while Sephardic Jews have roots in Spain, Portugal, and Latin America. Mizrahi Jews are from Asia and North Africa.

Empires and Occupations

Southwest Asia and North Africa have seen empires come and go over thousands of years. Each empire has left its mark on the culture and language of the people living there. While several different Arabic empires ruled parts of the region beginning in the seventh century, most of the land fell to the Turkey-based Ottoman Empire in the 15th century. Many European countries also **colonized** parts of the region in the 19th century to try to control the flow of **fossil fuels**. After World War I, European powers divided up the region, drawing many of today's borders and controlling the new states until the 1950s, when a wave of Arab **nationalism** largely brought the land back under native leadership.

In addition to the ethnic groups that make up the majority of people in each country, there are many different minority groups as well. These peoples include Azerbaijanis (who form a large minority in northern Iran and the majority in the neighboring nation, the Republic of Azerbaijan), Armenians, Yezidis (who live mostly in Iraq, as well as in Syria and Turkey), and Amazigh (an **indigenous** people of North Africa, also known as Berbers). There are also several minority cultures within the larger Arabic group, including religious **sects** such as the Alawites, who held power in the Syrian government in the 2010s, and the Bedouin, a group of **nomadic** people who have moved all around southwest Asia and North Africa throughout history.

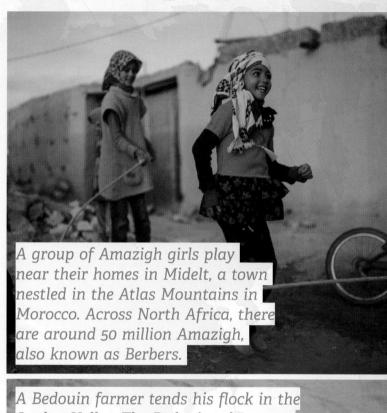

A group of Amazigh girls play near their homes in Midelt, a town nestled in the Atlas Mountains in Morocco. Across North Africa, there are around 50 million Amazigh, also known as Berbers.

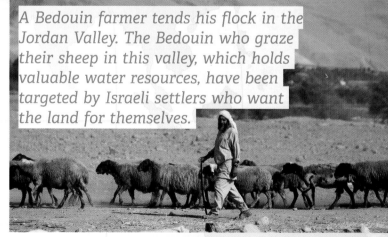

A Bedouin farmer tends his flock in the Jordan Valley. The Bedouin who graze their sheep in this valley, which holds valuable water resources, have been targeted by Israeli settlers who want the land for themselves.

2 THE BIRTHPLACE OF THREE FAITHS

Southwest Asia is the birthplace of three major world religions. Judaism, Christianity, and Islam are all based on **monotheism** and have spread widely around the world. However, Islam is the faith most people associate with the region. It is the religion most widely practiced among people in southwest Asia and North Africa, and its influence reaches deep into many societies there. In countries such as Saudi Arabia and Iran, it's an official state religion and the basis for national laws. In other nations, such as Turkey and Lebanon, Islam is simply an important element in the overall culture.

The Region's Religions

	JUDAISM ✡	CHRISTIANITY ✝	ISLAM ☪
COMMON SYMBOL			
FOLLOWERS	Jewish People	Christians	Muslims
KEY PERSON/PEOPLE	Abraham and Moses	Jesus	Muhammad
HOLY BOOK	The Torah	The Bible	The Qur'an
HOLY PLACE	Western Wall	Sepulchre	Mecca
PLACE OF WORSHIP	Synagogue	Church	Mosque
MAIN BRANCHES	Reformed, Conservative, Orthodox	Protestant, Catholic, Orthodox	Shia, Sufi, Sunni

Islam was founded in the Arabian Peninsula, in what is now Saudi Arabia, in the seventh century AD. Muhammad is a key figure in the religion: Muslims believe he was a prophet, or messenger, of Allah (God). He was born in Mecca around AD 570. After receiving a religious vision, Muhammad began to spread the word of Allah, written down in a book called the Qur'an. He eventually drew a large following.

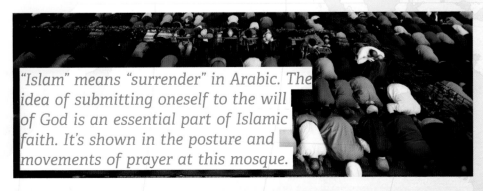

"Islam" means "surrender" in Arabic. The idea of submitting oneself to the will of God is an essential part of Islamic faith. It's shown in the posture and movements of prayer at this mosque.

Judaism in the Middle East

Like Islam, Judaism is founded on a belief in one god. Judaism was the earliest monotheistic faith to rise out of southwest Asia, around 2000 BC. Christianity and Islam grew out of its traditions. Both incorporate its holy book, the Torah, into their own religious literature. Israel and Jerusalem are a major part of Judaism, but after the Roman Empire expelled the Jews from Palestine in the first century AD, Jews existed primarily as the **Diaspora**, living outside of their place of origin. Upon the establishment of Israel in 1948, large Jewish communities in Europe—as well as in Morocco, Egypt, Syria, Iraq, and Yemen—moved to the new Jewish state. Significant Jewish communities still exist in Iran, Turkey, and Tunisia.

When Muhammad died, his work was carried on by four caliphs, or **successors**, who continued expanding the community of Islam throughout the Arabian Peninsula. During the seventh and eighth centuries AD, Arab armies of the Umayyad and Abbasid Dynasties conquered much of southwest Asia, North Africa, the Iberian Peninsula, and Central Asia, spreading their faith as they established control.

CULTURAL CONNECTIONS

Islam prohibits practices that are harmful to the body, mind, soul, or society. These prohibited acts, called haram, include eating pork, drinking alcohol, gambling, and killing.

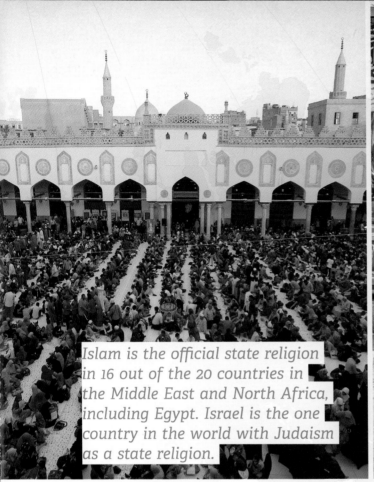

Islam is the official state religion in 16 out of the 20 countries in the Middle East and North Africa, including Egypt. Israel is the one country in the world with Judaism as a state religion.

Muslim and Jewish practices require eating meat that is butchered and blessed in a particular way.

The primary religious duties for Muslims are called the Five Pillars of Islam. These pillars are: the declaration of faith (*shahada*), prayer (*salat*), charity (*zakat*), fasting (*sawm*), and pilgrimage to Mecca (*hajj*).

CULTURAL CONNECTIONS

In addition to the three major religions, there are several prominent minority religions in the region, including Zoroastrianism, Baha'i, and Druze.

Christian Communities

While Jews believe that the Messiah—a holy king—will come at the end of time to redeem God's people, Christians believe that the Messiah already arrived in the form of Jesus Christ, the son of God. Christianity spread throughout the world thanks to Europe's Holy Roman Empire, but there are still strong Christian communities in the land of the religion's birth. The largest such community is that of the Coptic Christians in Egypt, who make up around 10 percent of the country's population, while Maronite Christians hold a great deal of political power in Lebanon. Other significant Christian communities can be found in Syria, Jordan, the West Bank, and Iraq.

Baha'i, which developed in Iraq in the 19th century, promotes peace, equality, and the unity of all religions. Its worldwide headquarters is in Haifa, Israel.

One core value of the religion is surrendering to the will of Allah, and prayer is a way of life for most Muslims. Faithful Muslims worship five times a day, with prayers at dawn, noon, midafternoon, sunset, and evening. These prayers can be performed anywhere, with the worshipper turned to face in

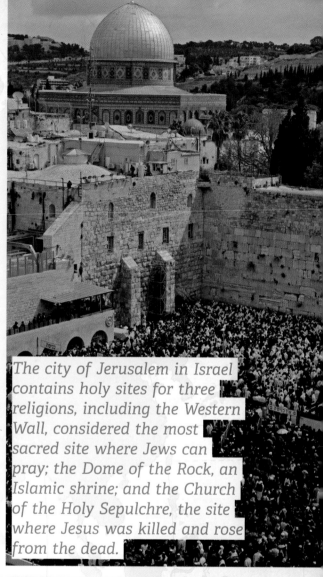

The city of Jerusalem in Israel contains holy sites for three religions, including the Western Wall, considered the most sacred site where Jews can pray; the Dome of the Rock, an Islamic shrine; and the Church of the Holy Sepulchre, the site where Jesus was killed and rose from the dead.

the direction of Mecca. A distinctive sound throughout southwest Asia and North Africa is the call to prayer, sounded from the **minarets** of mosques as the **muezzin** reminds Muslims of their duty to keep God in mind as they go about their days.

3 FEASTING AND FASTING

I slamic holidays are occasions for great public celebrations, feasts, and private reflection across southwest Asia and North Africa.

One of the most important religious occasions is the holy month of Ramadan, the ninth month of the Islamic calendar. This is the month in which the Qur'an was revealed to Muhammad. For the entire month, Muslims are required to fast, or not eat food and drink, during the day. The act of fasting, one of the

CULTURAL CONNECTIONS

Muslims who are sick, pregnant, nursing, or under the age of 12 can be excused from fasting during Ramadan, though adults are expected to make up for the fast later or donate to the poor instead.

five pillars of Islam, provides an opportunity for quiet reflection, self-discipline, focus on Allah and the Qur'an, and empathy for those less fortunate. Ramadan is also an important time to practice *zakat*, or charity, and communities often collect money and supplies for those in need during this time.

Construction workers in Dubai, United Arab Emirates, wait to break the Ramadan fast together with the evening meal called iftar.

Days of Awe

Fasting is also a central part of the Jewish holiday of Yom Kippur, the Day of Atonement. Along with Rosh Hashanah—the Jewish New Year—Yom Kippur is one of the High Holidays, the most sacred days in the Jewish calendar. In the spring, Jews honor their people's escape from ancient Egypt during Passover, which is celebrated with a meal called a seder. Coptic Christians also fast with a restricted diet in the month before Christmas, which falls on January 7 in the Orthodox Christian Church. In Bethlehem, Israel, the city of Jesus's birth, thousands of pilgrims from around the world gather for the Christmas celebration and midnight Mass.

A Jewish man in Israel prepares for Passover by making matzo, a traditional bread eaten during the holiday.

Pope Tawadros II of the Coptic Church of Egypt leads the Easter Mass at Saint Mark's Cathedral in Cairo. Coptics, who account for about 10 percent of the Egyptian population, are the largest Christian community in the Middle East.

The traditional way to break the fast each day is by sipping water and eating dates at sunset. This is followed by a meal called iftar. These meals can be large and festive, and many mosques and gathering places across the region set up tables offering free food for people to enjoy together in public.

CULTURAL CONNECTIONS

Islam uses a calendar based on the cycle of the moon instead of the solar Gregorian calendar, which most of the world uses to keep track of dates. Because the lunar year is shorter than the solar one, Muslim holidays come around 11 days earlier each solar year.

When Ramadan ends and the new month of Shawwal begins, Muslims go to the mosque for prayers and then gather with family and friends to celebrate Eid al-Fitr, or the Festival of Breaking Fast. In addition to giving gifts to mark the holiday, people also donate food to the poor, a donation called Zakat al-Fitr, so that every Muslim can celebrate.

Ringing in the Spring

In addition to the religious holidays, many **secular** and national holidays are observed across the region. In Egypt, the festival of Sham el-Nessim celebrates the beginning of springtime. People in Kuwait celebrate the arrival of spring's flowers and greenery in the desert with Hala, a month-long festival held in February. With roots in an ancient Zoroastrian holiday honoring the renewal of spring, Nowrūz is now widely known as the Persian New Year—though it's celebrated far beyond Iran's borders. Families celebrate Nowrūz with poetry, traditional songs, and feasts.

A woman in Tehran, Iran, jumps over a bonfire as part of the celebration during Nowrūz, which celebrates the arrival of spring.

Another major Muslim holiday is based on the **pilgrimage** to Mecca, called the hajj, which recreates the journey Muhammad took back to his birthplace in AD 632. Islamic law states that every Muslim who is physically and financially able is required to make the journey to Mecca at least once in their life. During the six days of the hajj, millions of pilgrims from all over the world come to Mecca to pray. At the end of the hajj, Muslims celebrate Eid al-Adha, the Festival of Sacrifice. This holiday, which can last for several days, honors Abraham. It's often celebrated with the sacrifice of a goat or lamb, whose meat is shared with friends, relatives, and the needy.

Pilgrims worship in Mecca, Saudi Arabia, during the hajj. Every year, millions of Muslims travel to the city to pray around the Kaaba, a black cube-shaped shrine believed to have been built by Abraham and his son Ismail.

pilgrimage: A journey to a sacred place.

The Hajj Guide

For Muslims, hajj is the fifth and final pillar of Islam. It takes place in the month of Dhul Hijjah, which is the twelfth month of the Islamic lunar calendar. Hajj officially begins on the eighth day of Dhul Hijjah and lasts for five days.

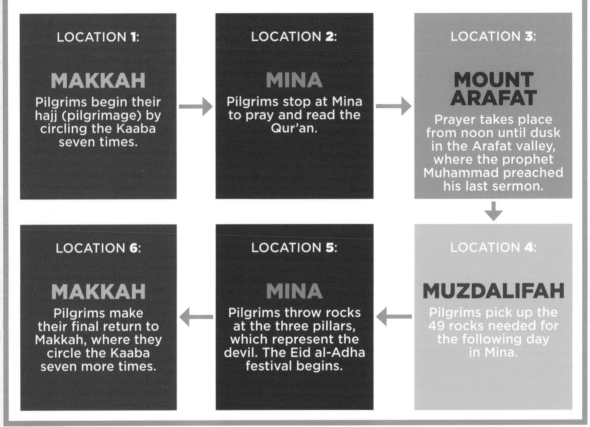

LOCATION 1:

MAKKAH

Pilgrims begin their hajj (pilgrimage) by circling the Kaaba seven times.

LOCATION 2:

MINA

Pilgrims stop at Mina to pray and read the Qur'an.

LOCATION 3:

MOUNT ARAFAT

Prayer takes place from noon until dusk in the Arafat valley, where the prophet Muhammad preached his last sermon.

LOCATION 6:

MAKKAH

Pilgrims make their final return to Makkah, where they circle the Kaaba seven more times.

LOCATION 5:

MINA

Pilgrims throw rocks at the three pillars, which represent the devil. The Eid al-Adha festival begins.

LOCATION 4:

MUZDALIFAH

Pilgrims pick up the 49 rocks needed for the following day in Mina.

This map lays out the holy sites to be visited and actions to be taken by the millions of Muslims who come to Mecca as part of the hajj pilgrimage.

CULTURAL CONNECTIONS

The COVID-19 global pandemic, which started in 2019, challenged the health, daily lives, religious customs, and celebrations of people in this region and the wider world.

4

WOMEN'S RIGHTS AND ROLES

The protection of women's rights in the Western world is sometimes taken for granted. In parts of southwest Asia and North Africa, on the other hand, women have far fewer protections, which vary based on their location, culture, and economic status. Some restrictions that women in the region face are a matter of local custom passed down through generations and enforced by families. Others are set in place by religious or national law.

The deeply religious nations of this region restrict many aspects of women's lives, but Islam itself gives women certain rights. These include the right to inherit, to work outside the home, and to be educated. According to the Qur'an, men and women are equal in the eyes of Allah. However, some **patriarchal** societies have interpreted the Qur'an in ways that reduce women's rights and status. Women often face social pressure to stay home with family instead of entering the workforce, receive unequal inheritance and property rights, and are subject to laws saying what they can wear and who they can marry.

Yemeni journalist and human rights activist Tawakkul Karman was one of three women to share the Nobel Peace Prize in 2011. The first Arab woman to win the prize, she was honored for her fight for free speech.

CULTURAL CONNECTIONS

Tunisia discourages women from wearing head coverings, and women in Turkey aren't allowed to wear religious head coverings in public offices or universities in an effort to promote a more secular society.

A restaurant in Saudi Arabia features two separate entrances: one for "singles" (or men), and one for "families," which includes women. Until December 2019, Saudi law demanded strict separation of men and women in public spaces.

Modesty is an important principle in Muslim cultures in the region, and tight-knit extended families expect relatives to maintain a good reputation. Men and women are generally discouraged from romantic interaction before marriage. In more religiously **conservative** areas, men and women who aren't married or close relatives avoid all physical contact–and in some cases will not even socialize together. This can limit women's participation in public life and the workforce.

CULTURAL CONNECTIONS

Modesty, particularly for women, is also a key value among Orthodox Jews in Israel. In addition to wearing modest clothes, Orthodox Jewish women who are married cover their hair, either with scarves called *mitpachat* or with wigs called sheitels.

conservative: Tending to stick to traditional ideas.

Maintaining Modesty

In Islam, one well-known expression of modesty in women is wearing a veil or head covering known as the hijab. This covering can take many forms. In the Gulf region, the popular style is the *shayla*, a long scarf wrapped around the head and fastened at the shoulders. In Iran, many women wear a full-body cloak called a chador. Saudi Arabia's strict dress code for women includes a long cloak called an abaya paired with a face covering called a niqab. While outsiders sometimes regard the hijab as merely a symbol of oppression, many women value the sense of privacy the veil offers.

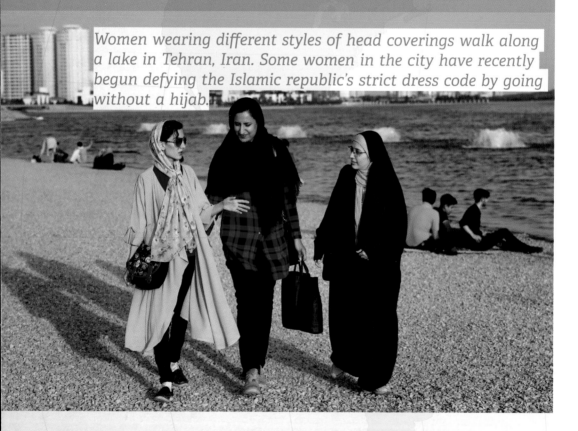

Women wearing different styles of head coverings walk along a lake in Tehran, Iran. Some women in the city have recently begun defying the Islamic republic's strict dress code by going without a hijab.

Women's educational opportunities were once limited in many countries in the region, but recent decades have seen this change somewhat. In Palestine, Libya, Tunisia, Kuwait, and the United Arab Emirates, university enrollment rates for women are slightly higher than for men. In Qatar, twice as many women are enrolled in universities as men.

When Did Women Receive Voting Rights in the Middle East?

AFGHANISTAN 1965	MOROCCO MAY 1963
ALGERIA JULY 5, 1962	OMAN 1997
BAHRAIN OCTOBER 24, 2002	QATAR 1999
EGYPT JUNE 23, 1956	SAUDI ARABIA 2015
IRAN SEPTEMBER 1963	SUDAN NOVEMBER 1964
IRAQ 1958	SYRIA SEPTEMBER 10, 1949
ISRAEL MAY 15, 1948	TUNISIA 1957
JORDAN 1974	TURKEY APRIL 3, 1930
KUWAIT VOTING PROHIBITED	UNITED ARAB EMIRATES 2006
LEBANON 1952	YEMEN 1967
LIBYA 1963	

In 1930, Turkey became the first country in the region to give women the right to vote. Saudi Arabia was the last, in 2011—though it wasn't until 2015 that there was an election in which women could exercise this right.

Saudi Arabia

Saudi Arabia—one of the world's richest countries thanks to its huge oil reserves—has also been one of the most oppressive when it comes to women's rights. The kingdom of Saudi Arabia follows an extremely conservative form of Islam called Wahhabism. While the government has begun to implement some reforms, women and men have traditionally been strictly **segregated** in public, and women couldn't associate with men who weren't close relatives. Until 2018, women were not allowed to drive in Saudi Arabia, and until 2019, a woman wasn't allowed to marry, get a passport and travel abroad, or leave prison without permission from her father, husband, or another male relative.

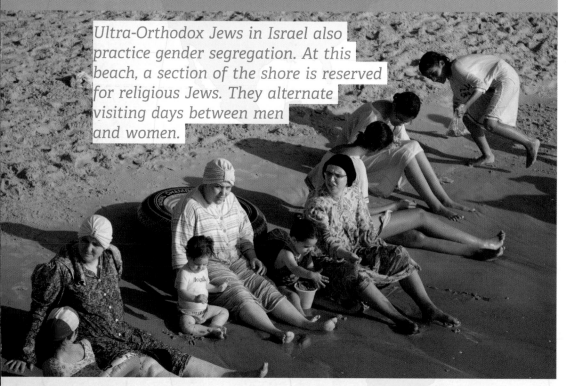

Ultra-Orthodox Jews in Israel also practice gender segregation. At this beach, a section of the shore is reserved for religious Jews. They alternate visiting days between men and women.

segregated: Separated based on race, class, or ethnicity.

With increased educational opportunities, women across the region are gaining more equality in other areas. In the business world, one in three **start-ups** in the region is founded or led by a woman. Women are also gaining ground in politics. Women currently hold an average of about 17.5 percent of national **parliament** seats in the region, up from just 4.3 percent in 1995. The cities of Baghdad, Tunis, and Bethlehem have all elected female mayors.

Young women seeking work take part in a job-training session in Jordan. Women of the region are entering the workforce in greater numbers.

5
ARTISTIC TRADITIONS

Rich artistic traditions have thrived in southwest Asia and North Africa for thousands of years. Many of these artistic practices have been influenced and inspired by Islam, while others draw on ancient folk traditions or a more **globalized** secular culture.

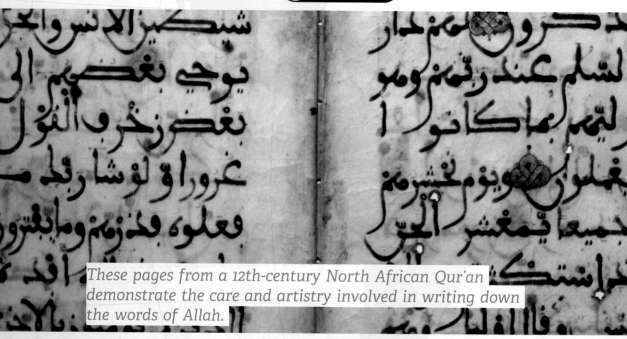

These pages from a 12th-century North African Qur'an demonstrate the care and artistry involved in writing down the words of Allah.

Islamic respect for the word of Allah—as recorded in the Qur'an—is reflected in the art of detailed handwriting called calligraphy, which many Muslims consider the most spiritually meaningful form of visual art. In addition to recreating Arabic verses from the Qur'an, calligraphy is also used to record other writings, such as blessings and poetry, and can be found decorating mosques, schools, and pottery.

Can Islamic Art Depict Living Things?

It's rare for Muslim artists to include images of people or animals in their work. It's a common myth that Islam forbids them from doing so—but it's more of a historical trend than a religious law. To avoid **idolatry**, most Muslim cultures don't show Muhammad, since the prophet himself isn't Allah. Under some extreme religious leaders, any representation of human and animal figures in art was forbidden because it was believed that only Allah can create living forms. Humans and animals do sometimes appear in traditional art from the region, but religious art and architecture generally use patterns made of geometric shapes and plants instead.

Persian mathematician Omar Khayyam, who lived from around 1048 to 1122, wrote poetry that combined philosophical ideas and verse.

Love for the written word isn't limited to calligraphy and religious literature. The region's ancient traditions of lengthy and songlike poetry have continued into the modern age. In the past century, writers from southwest Asia and North Africa have produced novels that record modern life and social change, including Mahmoud Saeed's *Saddam City* in 2004.

CULTURAL CONNECTIONS

One of the most popular types of music in North Africa is a Moroccan folk style called *gnawa*, which is based on the traditions of sub-Saharan Africans who arrived in Morocco as part of the slave trade.

Architecture has provided another outlet for Muslim artists in southwest Asia and North Africa to express their faith. There are grand historic places of worship, such as the eighth-century Umayyad Mosque in Damascus, Syria. More modern structures include Abu Dhabi's Sheikh Zayed Grand Mosque. Throughout the region there are humble madrasas (religious schools).

The intricate geometric patterns, stained glass, and colorful tile work of Istanbul's Sultan Ahmed Mosque demonstrate the common features of Islamic architecture.

Jewish architects who immigrated to Palestine from Germany brought with them the modernist Bauhaus style, which features modern materials, flat roofs, and simple colors.

No matter the size or scope, architecture in the region often features detailed geometric patterns that serve as a reminder of Allah's infinite nature. Both ancient and modern Islamic structures are well known for their gleaming tile work and **intricate** attention to detail.

CULTURAL CONNECTIONS

In recent decades, cinema has become an important form of artistic expression in the region. Iranian director Asghar Farhadi has won two Academy Awards for Best Foreign Language Film: *A Separation* in 2012 and *The Salesman* in 2016.

Textile arts, including silk designs, **embroidery**, block-printed cotton, and intricately woven carpets are still popular and widespread art forms in the region. Persian carpets, especially, are

Extremely detailed handwoven rugs are an important artistic and economic tradition across the region.

an important part of the economy of Iran, which shipped close to $100 million worth of these products to the United States in 2017.

Cultural Influences from Around the Globe

Southwest Asia and North Africa have always been realms of **cultural diffusion**. Conquering armies once spread Arab and Islamic culture through the region, while the Christian armies of the Crusades brought elements of Islamic art back to Europe. Trade routes, including the Silk Road, spread scientific and philosophical ideas along with fabrics, spices, and musical instruments from Asia to Europe and back. In recent decades, the prosperous oil economies of the Persian Gulf states have created new avenues for cultural diffusion. For example, Saudi Arabia spreads conservative Islamic ideals by funding mosques abroad. The United Arab Emirates hosts communities of Western professionals as well as workers from poorer parts of Asia.

Many areas of southwest Asia and North Africa have experienced warfare, political instability, and religious conflict in recent decades. Thus, these are the subjects that often appear in modern art. Individuals living through these times of conflict are popular topics for artists to explore. Artists like Mohammed Ehsai use abstract forms that look like calligraphic letters but don't spell anything. This artwork taps into the region's religious history while looking toward its future.

Egyptian singer Umm Kulthum is one of the best-selling Middle Eastern artists of all time. She gave popular monthly concerts in Cairo that were broadcast live across the region for decades.

6 DEMOCRACIES AND UPRISINGS

A variety of government systems are in place across southwest Asia and North Africa, including **democracies**, such as Israel and Tunisia, and Saudi Arabia's absolute monarchy. **Authoritarian** leaders are in power in many states in the region, including Egypt and Syria. They may hold elections, but they limit the power of citizens to choose candidates or influence public policy. In the Islamic Republic of Iran, citizens can vote in elections for president and other political representatives, but a religious authority called the ayatollah, or supreme leader, holds the most power over the state and daily life.

authoritarian: Concentrating power in a leader not constitutionally responsible to the people.

democracy: A government in which every person has a free and equal right to participate.

The economy of the Middle East is heavily dependent on oil production, and OPEC meetings, such as this one, force countries to put aside their differences to cooperate.

In any authoritarian system, governments maintain power by controlling information. Freedom of the press has been severely limited across the region, particularly in Yemen, Iran, Saudi Arabia, and Syria. State-operated news media sources shut out anyone who speaks out against the state. The growth of the internet

CULTURAL CONNECTIONS

Though Iran and Saudi Arabia follow different branches of Islam, they work together with other nations as part of the Organization of the Petroleum Exporting Countries **(OPEC)**. This association was formed in 1960 to make countries with a lot of oil reserves more powerful.

OPEC: A multinational group formed to coordinate worldwide petroleum policy and prices.

Cultural Collisions

The diversity of peoples and cultures in southwest Asia and North Africa hasn't always been an easy mix. Civil wars and conflicts between and within nations make constant news headlines about the region. The State of Israel has fought five wars with its Arab neighbors since its creation as a Jewish nation in 1948. The **sectarian** divide between two branches of Islam—Sunni and Shi'a—has played a role in civil wars in Iraq and Syria and in an ongoing **cold war** between Iran and Saudi Arabia. While many blame these conflicts on cultural divisions, the true root of the problem is commonly as simple as power and control over land and natural resources.

has presented a major challenge to oppressive governments that try to control information. Social media, especially, has allowed citizens to have access to broader conversations about democracy and spread their demands for **human rights**.

In 2011, a series of antigovernment uprisings known as the Arab Spring took place across the region. These protests were organized and spread on social media by young people who were fed up with oppressive and corrupt leaders and poor economic conditions. In Tunisia, where the movement

human rights: Universal rights possessed by all people in the world because they're human beings.

sectarian: Relating to strong support for a religious or political group in conflict with other groups.

began, protestors successfully toppled the longstanding president Zine al-Abidine Ben Ali and created a new constitution with free and democratic elections.

A Camp for Peace

Tensions are high and tempers run hot when it comes to different religions in this region. The State of Israel is often at the center of conflict, as it is a Jewish nation surrounded and outnumbered by Islamic countries. In 1978, U.S. president Jimmy Carter negotiated a peace agreement between Egypt and Israel in the form of the Camp David Accords. The first of its kind between an Arab nation and Israel, the Camp David Accords laid a foundation on which future leaders have tried to build further peace agreements.

In 1978, Egyptian President Anwar el-Sadat, left, and Israeli Prime Minister Menachem Begin, right, signed the Camp David Accords. The peace deal wouldn't have been possible without the help of U.S. president Jimmy Carter, center.

Results of similar uprisings in other countries weren't as positive, however. In Egypt, protests in Cairo's Tahrir Square successfully removed President Hosni Mubarak, who had been in office for 30 years—but violent instability followed. While protestors succeeded in overturning governments in Libya and Yemen, the chaos ended in civil war, which also broke out in Iraq and Syria.

الدستور
أخيراتنحى

A demonstrator in Tahrir Square in Cairo, Egypt, holds up a newspaper announcing that longtime president Hosni Mubarak has finally stepped down.

Because of tweet
NABEEL RAJAB
was arrested

A human rights activist in Bahrain protests the arrest of a fellow activist who allegedly wrote insulting tweets. In the wake of the Arab Spring, Gulf State rulers cracked down on bloggers and online activists.

Though the results of the Arab Spring were mixed, the uprisings successfully showed the power of young people and a growing

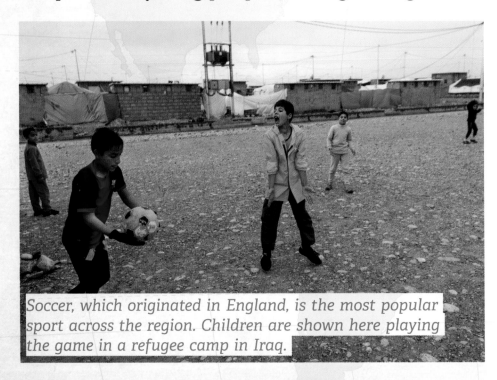

Soccer, which originated in England, is the most popular sport across the region. Children are shown here playing the game in a refugee camp in Iraq.

belief in free expression and democracy. The population of southwest Asia and North Africa is a very young one. Among the region's 370 million Arabs, the median age is 24. This new generation of young people in the region is better educated and more connected to the world than ever before. This generation is finding ways to combine its youthful voice with the region's rich history to improve life both locally and around the globe.

This map shows the countries that participated in the Arab Spring uprisings of 2011.

GLOSSARY

autonomous: Not controlled by others or outside forces.

cold war: A conflict between groups that doesn't involve actual fighting.

colonize: To establish a colony.

dialect: A form of language spoken in a certain area that uses some of its own words, grammar, and pronunciations.

idolatry: The worship of a physical object as a god.

indigenous: Describing groups that are native to a particular region.

minaret: A tall, slender tower of a mosque with one or more balconies from which the summons to prayer is cried.

muezzin: A Muslim crier who calls the hour of daily prayers.

parliament: The group of people who are responsible for making the laws in some kinds of government.

propaganda: Art, written materials, or ideas that are spread to support a government or cause and are often false or misleading.

sect: A small religious group within a larger religion.

start-up: A new business.

FOR MORE INFORMATION

BOOKS:

Gitlin, Marty. *Peace in the Middle East*. New York, NY: Greenhaven Publishing, 2018.

Maxim, Bailey. *The Colonial and Postcolonial Middle East*. New York, NY: Britannica Educational Publishing, 2016.

Randolph, Joanne. *The Myths and Legends of the Middle East*. New York, NY: Cavendish Square Publishing, 2018.

WEBSITES:

Access Islam

www.thirteen.org/edonline/accessislam

This educational site about Islamic cultures and traditions features videos, timelines, and a glossary.

Global Connections: The Middle East

www.pbs.org/wgbh/globalconnections/mideast/questions/nations/index.html#democracy

This portal from PBS offers an in-depth look at the history of the Middle East and an exploration of cultural and political issues.

TeachMideast

teachmideast.org

This educational initiative of the Middle East Policy Council has guides to various topics and collects news and culture articles to promote a deeper understanding of the region.

Publisher's note to educators and parents: Our editors have carefully reviewed these websites to ensure that they are suitable for students. Many websites change frequently, however, and we cannot guarantee that a site's future contents will continue to meet our high standards of quality and educational value. Be advised that students should be closely supervised whenever they access the internet.

INDEX